The Music in the Streets

The music in the streets

Fred Wilde

Prefatory Note by Sir John Betjeman

Collins
8 Grafton Street, London W1
1983

William Collins Sons & Co Ltd
London · Glasgow · Sydney · Auckland
Toronto · Johannesburg

First published 1983

Reprinted 1983

© Fred Wilde

Produced for Collins by the Cupid Press
2 Quay Street, Woodbridge, Suffolk

Designed by John and Griselda Lewis

Made and printed in Great Britain by
W. S. Cowell Ltd, Ipswich

Most of the paintings were photographed for this book by Derrick E. Witty

British Library Cataloguing in Publication Data

Wilde, Fred
The music in the streets.
1. Rochdale(Greater Manchester) – Social life and customs
1. Title
942.7'392 DA690.R55

ISBN 0-00-217169-4

Contents

FRED WILDE

Bury Times March 1982

Prefatory Note by Sir John Betjeman

I love Fred Wilde's beautiful book, *The Clatter of Clogs in the Early Morning*. His new book, *The Music in the Streets*, is equally good, full of a tremendous sense of atmosphere and of time past but still well remembered by some of us. Mr Wilde is an artist indeed.

The Mantelpiece

Draped with swagged and bobbled chenille or plush, above the high black grate, was the mantelpiece, a high shelf where things were safe from little prying hands. Here t'Royal Liver Club books and money could be left in safety, to be collected by t'club fella. Here unanswered letters could be filed until the ink-bottle and Waverley pen could be found and a tongue-in-mouth-corner reply be tardily penned. Dad's pipe had its special place here; so did the reading glass he used because he was perhaps too vain to wear spectacles.

Apart from all the odds and ends of daily living that one had to put one's hand on readily this was also a place for ornaments and family heirlooms, such as the Staffordshire dogs – King Charles spaniels, gold-collared, chained and padlocked – the romantic pottery figures of Dick Turpin and Tom King, and the oval prints of grandad and grandma, one on each side of the black marble clock.

Grate Day

Under the mantelpiece was the high, black grate, with the bread oven, and the brass-tapped hot water tank alongside the fire. Often the water was slightly rust-coloured, but never so bad that it could not be used for the Friday-night-in-front-of-the-fire bath.

Thursday was baking day, and on every Friday morning the pegged hearth-rug would be turned back, revealing the flag-stones below. The steel fender and fire-irons were taken out and stood up in the corner, and it was my job to clean these every week with near worn-out emery paper. (But I was never allowed to touch the brass fire-irons and fender that graced the parlour.)

Then the fire would be allowed to die down and the whole grate would be elbow-greased with shiny black lead. And on Friday nights we had our baths in front of the fire.

The Last of the Summer Wine

Mother, who regarded anything 'shop-bought' as rubbish, not only baked her own bread, pies and cakes, and made her own jams and pickles. She also made her own wine, which was quite famous amongst our neighbours.

The last of the summer wine to be made was elderberry. The berries grew for free, in dark royal clusters in the vineyard of the local hedgerows, smelling of high summer. Twelve pounds or so made three gallons of nectar, rich, dark and potent.

They were crushed until the juice ran in the large earthenware bread-crock, by vigorous wielding of the potato-masher, and soon the kitchen was filled with the rich smell of running juice. The sugar came from blue paper bags (of which the rough side was good for chalk drawings). The necks of the bags were tied up with thin, hairy string known as 'sugar-bant'. After the sugar was added the baker's barm was toast-rafted on the surface. Then the whole concoction, covered with a cloth to keep out the dust, was placed in the hearth where it fermented and quietly bubbled like a friendly witch's cauldron.

Afterwards it was bottled and put away to mature, unless a cork flew out with a pop or, as sometimes happened, the bottle burst with a shattering report. But by and large the brew matured into a drink fit for Olympus, a thick, rich potion that could just as effectively have dyed a Caesar's toga.

Dancing in the Rain

Collars and umbrellas are up, and everyone seems to be hurrying home. It's the sort of night when people say 'It's not fit to turn the dog out'.

But I have surprisingly happy memories of evenings like this, when I was small, holding Mum's hand on one side and Dad's on the other, as we trudged through the darkness and the rain. For the lighted gas-lamps seemed more beautiful than ever, each with its snaky reflection and halo of slanting golden drops. The cobblestones not only sparkled but seemed to be dancing.

In the far distance were the Pennines, which had seen it all a thousand times before, and their ancient back-cloth seemed to add a touch of drama to the storm.

But all my Mum and Dad were thinking about, I fancy, was the number of steps before we reached home, and the cold rain seeping down inside their collars.

Matt Woodhead's Pea-Soup Tent

I only remember it being there in cold weather; but I suppose it was there all the time, standing at the far end of the market square, alongside Buffalo Bill's Rough Riders. It was a brightly striped tent, with the bare market cobblestones for floor.

Matt had two set-boilers, like the one Mum used at home for boiling the whites on a Monday morning. In these he concocted his black-pea soup and his mushy-peas. Both of these delicacies, along with tripe, cow-heels, pigs' trotters and black puddings, were for consumption on the premises.

I was mostly interested in the black-pea soup, though now and again I enjoyed a hot black pudding, with mustard, sandwiched between a fresh oven-bottom muffin. The black peas were known politely as maple peas – or on the east coast, carlins. They were steeped overnight and then boiled with hambones and onions. I bought them by the bowl-ful, adding salt and vinegar to taste. The vinegar turned the rich gravy into a kind of jelly. After many years I still imagine I can taste it. I wish I knew where I could get some.

The Music in the Streets

Between the wars, when unemployment in Lancashire was as swingeing as it is now, but the relief was scanty, the streets were alive with musicians – if that is not too grand a name for them.

Many of these were ex-soldiers who had returned from the Great War (the first one, that is) and sought in vain for the promised 'land fit for heroes'. They joined up as curb-shuffling orchestras, with cornet, drum and accordion, accompanying throaty singers who rendered 'Roses are blooming in Picardy'.

Some of them, however, were buskers by choice: theatre-queue entertainers, whose accompaniment might be a gramophone in a pram, and whose partners were sometimes Dancing Bears. (I often wondered where the Bears spent their nights. Who would be eager to give a Bear bed-and-breakfast?)

The most familiar of all was the barrel-organ grinder, who churned out his plink-plonk melodies with practised flicks of the wrist. His repertoire tended to be distinctly pre-war (pre First-War, I mean). Favourites were *Alexander's Ragtime Band* and *Lily of Laguna*. He often had a pair of red-jacketed monkeys. Like little gone-wrong men they clambered with enviable agility over the canvas-covered instrument, holding out to onlookers their little tin cups into which pennies fell with a clink.

I used to long to touch them, and stroke them, but I didn't dare. They were alien and strange, and they had yellow teeth.

The Muffin Man

Down the street came the Muffin Man, announcing himself with voice and handbell. Once or twice a week he came, with his head-load of delicious wares – pikelets and crumpets as well as muffins.

I am not sure what exactly is the difference between pikelets and crumpets, but I am certain of one thing – that any one of them, toasted before a red fire on a dark winter's afternoon, and eaten hot, its surface pits brimming with 'best' butter, is a treat for the gods.

Stop to consider another feature of the Muffin Man and his place in the scheme of things. He *made* his muffins and crumpets and pikelets, and he *sold* them, and he *delivered* them to the customer. He was a totally self-sufficient, self-supporting, one-man concern.

Oh, where are you now, Muffin Man?

Shedding the Light

Then, as now, the Salvation Army was always active with its good works; and on Saturday evenings it 'shed the light' with the aid of stirring hymn tunes, the beat firmly maintained by the big base drum, and the tambourines tinkling in and out of the melodies. The tambourines were also, of course, very useful for collecting cash, which was one of the main aims of the performance.

The phrase 'shedding the light' in my mind meant not so much the light of the Gospel as the gaslight shed over the assembled throng from the lampost in the street.

While the Sun Shines

For the farmer hay-making and harvest are his moments of truth. The sun is his arbiter. For the children it is something quite different. No longer is a hay field a standing meadow, a forbidden place; it is somewhere where they can bury themselves in scented heaps, and toss armfuls of drying grass and scented flowers from one to the other. It is almost as good as playing on the sands.

Meanwhile the grown-ups, the gatherers, not only make hay while the sun shines but work on into the warm twilight to stack and store what earth and sun have given them.

The Challenge Match

Regularly the local papers contained announcements of challenges to running or walking contests. 'Albert Wakefield will walk against all comers over a ten-mile agreed flat course, for £5 a man, winner take all. Match to be made at *The Throstle's Nest* next Friday, 8 to 10 p.m.' This sort of challenge was irresistable to the more robust members of the community, and there was no lack of competitors who 'fancied their chance'. The matches always started and finished at a pub.

In the centre of the group is Albert, wearing braces and long shorts (or short longs). His challengers include farm labourers, footballers, and an ex-sailor. The landlord of *T'Nest*, Johnny Tagg, wearing his best blue-serge suit, is starter, stake-holder, referee and time-keeper.

Albert is complaining of the place he has been given. 'Tha allus puts me i' t'front of t'bloody puddles'. To which Johnny replies, 'If tha doesna' stop thi belly-achin Ah shall disqualify thee'.

In *The Sporting Life* challenges were sometimes issued to 'run any man for two hours from one mile to twenty' at Liverpool or Edinburgh for stakes as high as £30.

The Red Lions

Another form of sport was, of course, football, especially as more and more mills ceased to work on Saturday afternoons. Several of the larger pubs got up their own football teams, which competed in the local leagues such as 't'Sat'day Combination'. The *Red Lion* had a flourishing team, though most of their players were past their willowy best, for 'brewer's droop' is no respecter of waist-lines. But in their time they had been good enough to win 't'Cup' and to have engaged Snapper Searle to record the fact for posterity.

Inevitably several large, double-alberted gentlemen managed to work their way into the picture, some officially as Manager, Assistants or Trainer. The latter's gladstone bag of office, containing embrocation (pungent and penetrating), elastic bandages, sticking plaster and sponge, along with a bucket of cold water and turkish towel, were all the first aids he had with which to carry out running repairs. There were no painkilling aerosols in those days.

Hero-worshipping small boys sought to achieve fame by peeping through the arches of grown-up legs, but Willie Connor's dog got a front seat . . . it would!

Ten to Win and the Last Man In

At top level cricket was a Gentleman's game. Professionals were merely recorded in the score books with their surnames; amateurs were allowed the privilege of having initials as well. It was supposed to be a character-building game, and our school teacher celebrated its honourable competitiveness by quoting splendid lines of verse about 'a bumping pitch and a blinding light', with 'ten to win and the last man in'.

Our local game was not played quite on this level. We tried to pick the wrong'un amongst the hummocks and cow-flops, but the situation could be just as tense as on the playing fields of Eton.

Owd 'Juddy' Ollerenshaw, blacksmith and demon bowler, is just coming in to bat, complete with braces and off-white regalia. He will take 'middle-and-leg, please', but he is not noted for his finesse. He is capable of hitting the first two balls out of the ground to gain a glorious victory. But a subtle leg-break may well weave its way past his flailing bat.

Whatever happens, he can be relied upon to 'play the game' and if he argues with the umpire it will be under his breath.

Hambleton's Pond

Fishing (the common, coarse, variety) was more than an obsession with me, it was a sort of natural religion. I ate, slept and dreamed fishing, as did my special friend Willie and, to a lesser extent, Harry.

Saturdays and Hambleton's pond were the favourite combination. There we would select our 'fishy pegs' and bait up with maggots or soft new bread on minute 18s hooks, and try to catch the wary, small Crucian Carp, which were round-bodied and fat, and shone like newly minted gold. We fished also for the tiny silver-bright, red-finned Roach with their big orange eyes.

The Carp were readily marketable, for they throve in garden ponds, and were worth a penny or twopence apiece, according to size. The Roach we returned, after keeping them in our large bait-can until the end of the session. There were undernourished, greedy, prickle-finned Perch in there as well, but they were so eager for food that they almost gave themselves up. They 'bided' no catching; so we didn't rate them very highly.

Oh! those were peaceful, magic days, when the world was full of fresh wonder and discovery; when each new morning heralded the best day since creation.

The only occasional fly in our ointment was a bull in the field. We were sure owd 'Ambleton let it out on purpose to spite us. When the bull *was* in the field you had to look out for yourself, and fishing was restricted to the corner near the gate in case of a bull-rush and the desperate need for a quick get-away.

Homer's Odyssey

The chief interest of many of the village worthies was and still is the gentle art of pigeon fancying. They had their lofts of champions, where the secrets of feeding and breeding and pigeon psychology were studied with total application and in maximum security. More often than not 'the wife' came a very poor second to the birds.

On short flights some of these winged sprinters could achieve more than a mile a minute, while others could, by some magical process, find their way home to the loft over hundreds of miles. Races from the Continent were regular events.

In the painting the proud fancier is basketing some of his long-distance birds, whose individual names and pedigrees he knows better than those of his own family. He is extolling the merits of one of his best thoroughbreds, a 'homer' beyond compare. I could do nothing else but name this painting 'Homer's Odyssey'.

Joys and Hazards of Wakes Week

Wakes Week was the one special week out of the fifty-two, when money was drawn out of the 'diddle-em' club at t'mill and half of it was promptly invested in railway fares and self-catering apartments at the seaside – with use of cruet.

No factory buzzers sounded of a morning for seven blissful days. The tyranny of Timekeeping was suspended – except for 'Opening Time' and 'Time, gentleman, please'.

And the sea was there, coming and going with its age-old rythmn, prompting a strange sense of liberation and adventure, reminding us – if we ever thought about it – that we are a seafaring nation. The sea stirred our street-bred blood into acts of reckless abandon. So roll up the 'keks', undo the suspenders, take off the socks and beetle-crushers, and let the gritty sand work its way between the corns and bunions on your toes. 'The brine will do them a world of good'.

But have a care! Don't let the ozone go to your head. Even though May is out, hesitate before you cast a clout. Retain the pot-'at, the braces and the high-necked, half-sleeved vest. You don't want to catch your death of cold. Time enough for shedding them if 't'weather keeps up'.

Pleasures of the Pier

'What the Butler Saw', 'Dad's Bit of Fluff', and other long-lasting, traditional peepshows on the pier have now become classics and have acquired an amusing kind of respectability. It is hard to believe that they were once regarded as pornographic, and highly 'unsuitable' for the young.

The do's and don'ts being slightly relaxed when on holiday, dare-devil or slightly 'depraved' youths used to drop their guilty pennies into the slot in order to join the butler in his Shocking Revelations of High Life or spy on the respected Edwardian paterfamilias as he visited his 'bit on the side'.

These jerky revelations had very little appeal for the girls, who were quickly bored by the goings-on, and quite deaf to the appeals of 'Eigh, come on!' This exhortation could have two meanings, though, for the three likely lads, in masher outfits of striped blazer, flannel trousers and straw cadeys, have succeeded in 'getting off' with the trio of questing girls.

'Eigh, come on! Mine's the one in blue'.

Don't Forget the Diver

Most years we spent our Wakes-Week holiday at Egremont, on the Wirral peninsula. It was a poor relation of the grander sea-side resort of New Brighton. We could not afford the flesh-pots of New Brighton, but we could, several times during the week, taste it's heady delights, for it was within walking distance. As a special treat we sometimes made the short trip by boat, catching one of the fussy, black-and-white, round-rumped ferry boats. Two of these boats had earned the prefix 'Royal' because of their part in the raid on Zeebrugge in 1918. They were the *Royal Daffodil* and the *Royal Iris*.

When we did go by boat one of the exciting things to look out for was the famous Diver. He was a daring, one-legged man who made death-defying dives from the height of New Brighton pier into the murky waters of the Mersey.

He timed his spectacular plunges with the arrival of the ferry-boat full of trippers, and his wife collected pennies from them by means of a bag on a long stick.

She would cry, 'Come on now. Don't forget the diver. Every penny makes the water warmer,' and, 'If you don't put a penny in the bag it'll rain before you go home tonight.'

After each dive he had to climb back up a narrow, iron companion ladder, his one leg making him hump up like a sea-lion. This impressed me almost as much as the dive.

Those of us old enough to remember the Liverpool comedian Tommy Handley, in the ITMA broadcasts during the last war, will remember that he didn't forget the diver either!

Won't Last Half an Hour

Rain and Lancashire – yes, they are always linked together. The legend persists, and we certainly get our share. But we get no more than a lot of places, and not so much as some. It has been said that the reason why the cotton industry settled in this part of the world was that cotton will not weave well unless it has a humid atmosphere, and that is something Lancashire can certainly provide.

And there is much beauty in rain, in the 'sunshiny shower' that 'won't last half an hour'. See how the light-dazzle reflects from the glistening cobbles and pavement-flags. It softens every hard edge between the eye and the light-source and is almost blinding to look at.

Once I had an idea that there was no pure white in nature. But here it is – pure light – a white to surpass the most boastful claims of the soap-powder people – and, yes I was right, impossible to paint!

Cobble-Dazzle

I read somewhere that the great Persian conqueror, Darius, wrote upon a rock near Hamadan a hymn to Amamazda, the god of light, 'who created mankind, who created the spirit of man', and who (needless to say) 'made Darius king'.

I don't take such a personal view of Amamazda, but what a wonderful thing light is! It can imbue the ordinary with beauty, and transform the mundane into the magnificent.

Look down at the cobble-stones. Goodness knows these are commonplace and utterly unromantic things, whose only purpose is to stand between feet and wheels and mother earth. Yet look at them after rain, when they take on a wonderful radiance, reflecting the sun like fresh-cut diamonds, and making flawed mirrors of the pavements.

City Lights

After the widely spaced gas lamps of the village street and the dim light that came from the windows of the village shops the City was a place ablaze with illumination.

The big, brash department stores were something out of another world. They sold everything from cheap tin toys to new-fangled bathrooms and complete housefuls of furniture. And it was all there to be touched if one wished.

The tall lamp standards in the streets seemed to stand as close to one another as trees in a wood, and many of them had electric lights, not gas-lamps.

It was high adventure to cross the street, for the traffic roared and never seemed to stop. On the pavements the crowds jostled and shoved, and nobody ever said 'Sorry'! One felt like a very small frog in a very large pond.

After an afternoon in the City it was good to be back in the quiet 'gobbin' life of the village, where the pond was not so big and everything felt familiar and secure. But at the back of one's mind was always the knowledge of that fascinating wonderland of City Lights, just a tram ride away down the road.

Saturday Matinee

Do you remember them – those queues for Saturday Matinees at the local 'laugh-and-scratch', waiting to get our weekly ration of action-packed, larger-than-life serials?

Will she be swept screaming over the waterfall? Will the lowering Fu-manchu ceiling perforate the hero with its thousand spikes? Will the Seventh Cavalry arrive in time, with their 'long knives' drawn and their bugles blowing? Find out next week!

Throughout the intervening days of the week we re-enacted all the incidents, with variations. 'I'm Eddie Polo'. 'Well, I'm Tom Mix'.

Next Saturday, standing outside the 'bug-hut', our pennies in our clammy hands, we let off steam and quelled our impatience by sparring and wrestling with our friends in pent-up boisterousness. Owd Sergeant-Major Grimshaw loudly admonished the unruly, cowing them with his threat 'If tha doesn'a stop thi mallokin ah's mek thi goo t'th'end o't'queue'.

Meeson's sweet shop was a godsend, with its 'Buy a quarter, get a quarter free'.

The Coming of the Talkies

Away with the wordless mouthings, the over-acting, and the written subtitles – 'Meanwhile back in the ranch' or 'Came the dawn'. Good-bye, too, to the ready-fingered pianist in the pit with his or her happy, sad, exciting or frightening accompaniments. For the all-singing, all-talking, all-dancing talkies are here – the wonder of the age!

Al Jolson has a rainbow round his shoulder and is inviting a tear-provoking Sonny Boy to climb on his knee. Now we can all hear, as well as see, the contrived dramas, the mirth-provoking comedies, and the audible news. Whatever next? Colour?

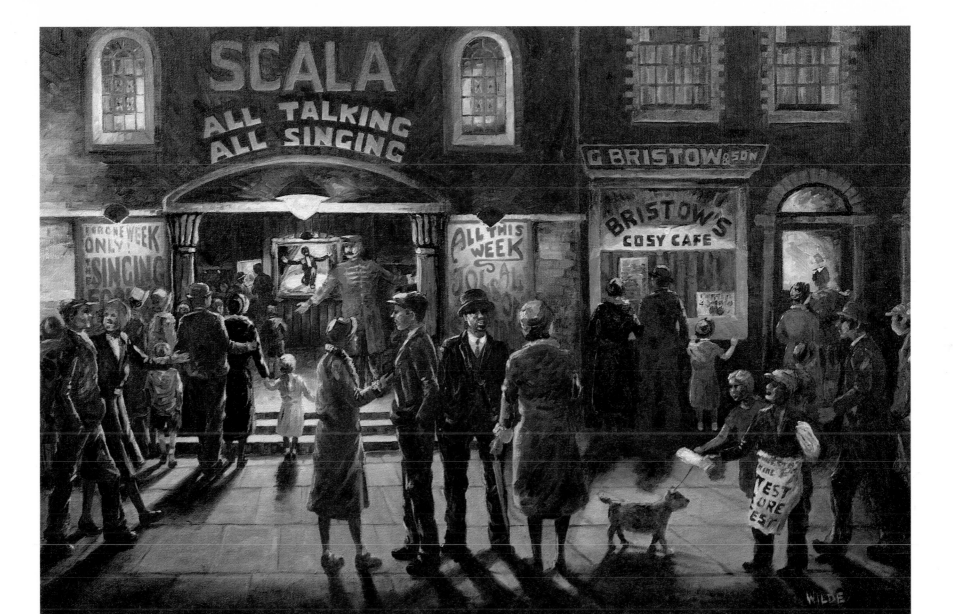

'Yes, when he's finished his practice'

At one stage in my childhood my Mum decided I had the makings of a concert pianist. Goodness knows why, for I hadn't got a note of music in my inky fingers. But then Mums often entertain impossible dreams for their sons.

Beside the aspidistra in our black-horse-haired, overstuffed parlour was an instrument of torture known as an upright iron grand. A piano teacher appeared, in the shape of owd 'Bottleneck' Hopkins, the choir-master from the church. He and his ally – *William Smallwood's Pianoforte Tutor* – struggled manfully with my musical education for a long time before Owd Bottleneck realised that life was too short and he could be more gainfully employed elsewhere.

Two more teachers followed, but I wore out both of them by way of the fumbling 'Bluebells of Scotland', 'Won't you buy my Pretty Flowers?' and chromatic scales – whatever they were! At last my Mum gave in, realizing my total incapacity to play, and she settled for me joining the choir. But I can still vividly remember the daily agony of those enforced, hour-long, finger-fumbling practices, especially on sunlit summer evenings, after school, when my pals would knock at the door, cricket bat and ball in hand, and ask 'Is your Freddie comin' out to play?'

The reply would always be: 'Yes, when he's finished his practice'.

Ginnels and Giddle-Gaddles

The correct and polite word is 'passage', or 'entry'. But to those that lived there they were known as 'ginnels', or, if they had a number of bends or corners, 'giddle-gaddles'.

On Merseyside, which was once quite a distinct part of Lancashire, they were known as 'jiggers', and were inhabited by 'jigger rabbits', which folk in the South know as 'moggies'.

Generally these ginnels or jiggers ran between the backs of terraced houses to give access to back-yards for deliveries of coal or other heavy goods or prams or bicycles. There were seldom any street lamps or any other form of lighting, so they were rather frightening places for small children at night. Perhaps this was just as well because they were largely populated by courting couples.

The graffiti on the walls were, as I remember, a lot simpler – 'Joe loves Ellen', etc. – and more innocent than those of today, but, I venture to assert, the spelling was much better.

Champion Courting Country

After dark the tow-path alongside the canal, known as the 'cut-side', was a favourite place for courting couples as it was shrouded in kindly conspiratorial gloom. The light of the sky was reflected, somewhat mysteriously, in the vague ribbon of water. The only illumination was by the bridges, where there were snake-like wriggles of lamplight in the water and shifting images of the windows in the mill.

But these beauties of the night were hardly noticed by the dog-walking husband, and not at all by the other frequenters of the cut-side. For this was champion courting country.

It's Never Quite the Same Again

There comes a magic moment in the life of most boys when, to their utter confusion, they realise that girls are more than just a soft sort of lad, something other than the species which only cissie boys play with.

All at once girls become something different. Some mysterious chemistry begins to tell a boy that this other sex, which until now he has viewed with scorn, is unique and rather special – particularly one exceptional girl. Most likely he will become clumsy and tongue-tied in her presence, and finds it difficult to say her name, though he can get great pleasure from endlessly writing it down in private. Nothing like this has happened to him before, and he has no clue as to what has overtaken him. All he knows is that the savour has gone out of bullhead fishing, and his old companions are no longer all-sufficient.

The odds are, though, that the girl knows *all* about it, and has done so for some time. You and I know this state as first love . . . and it's never the same again.

Meetin' the New Fella

After a certain amount of prompting and persuasion he has, with some misgivings, come to meet her parents for the first time. It is Sunday afternoon, and to say that he is desperately nervous is putting it mildly.

There he sits, solitary in the parlour, balanced on the edge of his chair, wearing his best brown suit, with his new straw-cadey in his lap. The family dog is sniffing round his trouser turn-ups, and he doesn't know if he is going to be accepted, nipped or peed on.

In the kitchen meanwhile a somewhat reluctant Father is being forced into a collar and tie, though he is full of Sunday best bitter, roast sirloin and Yorkshire pudding, and wants nothing more than to be left in peace to enjoy his customary forty winks.

Mum, rising naturally to the momentous occasion, is titivating in front of the mirror, and the twins are peeping and tittering audibly one to another. 'Ee! i'n't our Annie's fella funny!'

I can still feel the trauma of that afternoon, though it is from the other end of life.

The Pennine streams were once sweet, with clean soft water. But cotton demanded unlimited supplies of this gift of nature for spinning, weaving, bleaching, dyeing and printing. So t'mills were built, like grimy beads on threads of brooks. Often one mill would tap the overflow from the one above in its own reservoir or lodge. Each had its name on the chimney or tower, for they were proud men who built the mills and named them . . . Astley, Slack, Pear, Atlas, India, Gee-cross.

Fortunately the upper slopes of the hills and moors escaped the desecration that befell Cotton Valley, and they remained largely unspoilt. They are the lungs of Lancashire.

The artist is grateful to all those listed below for permission to reproduce paintings in their possession.

Mr and Mrs J. Brunton	Cotton Valley
Mr and Mrs G. Milton	The Mantelpiece
Mr and Mrs J. Burke	The Last of the Summer Wine
Mr and Mrs K. Smith	Dancing in the Rain
Mr and Mrs M. Holman	Matt Woodhead's Pea-Soup Tent
Mr and Mrs A. Crimlisk	The Music in the Streets
Mr and Mrs J. Reynard	The Muffin Man
Mr and Mrs D. Duxbury	Shedding the Light
Mr and Mrs E. G. Milton	While the Sun Shines
Edward Woodward and Michele Dotrice	The Challenge Match
Mr and Mrs G. Raynor	The Red Lions
Edward Woodward and Michele Dotrice	Ten to Win and the Last Man in
Mr and Mrs S. Birchall	Hambleton's Pond
Mr S. Binks	Homer's Odyssey
Mr and Mrs J. Flinn	Joys and Hazards of Wakes Week
Mr and Mrs J. Reynard	Pleasures of the Pier
Dr and Mrs J. Sugden	Won't Last Half an Hour
Mr and Mrs A. Dawson	Cobble-Dazzle
Mr and Mrs C. Payne	City Lights
Mr and Mrs A. Reynard	Saturday Matinee
Edward Woodward and Michele Dotrice	The Coming of the Talkies
Mr and Mrs E. Priestley	'Yes, when he's finished his practice'
Mrs A. Davenport	Ginnels and Giddle-Gaddles
Mr and Mrs M. Blond	Champion Courting Country
Mr and Mrs W. Flood	It's Never Quite the Same Again
Mr and Mrs Hamer	Meetin' the New Fella

FRED WILDE was born at Hyde, near Manchester, 'a long time ago', as he puts it. He was brought up in the shadow of the cotton mills. It was an environment in which there were few luxuries. Wireless was a novelty, a visit to 'the pictures' was an event; none of the neighbours owned a car; some had never seen the sea. As a young man Fred briefly attended Hyde Art School, and later he did some life drawings at Manchester Municipal Art School. But for many years his chief artistic activity was designing textiles for export to Africa. He retired from his job early in order to devote his time to painting scenes of his childhood 'between the wars'. His first book *The Clatter of Clogs in the Early Morning* (1982) became a best seller in Lancashire, and won praise from J. B. Priestley and Roger McGough. Fred now lives at Lydiate, north of Liverpool.